Praying Our Experiences

Praying Our Experiences

Twentieth Anniversary Expanded Edition

Joseph F. Schmidt, FSC

Foreword by Richard Rohr, OFM

Saint Mary's Press
Christian Brothers Publications
Winona, Minnesota

The publishing team included Carl Koch and Michael Wilt, development editors; Laurie A. Berg, copy editor; Lynn Dahdal, production editor and typesetter; Cären Yang, designer; pre-press, printing, and binding by the graphics division of Saint Mary's Press.

Cover photograph by Rachel Wood

Portions of this book previously appeared in *Praying* and *Review for Religious*.

Printed in the United States of America

Printing: 7 6 5 4 3 2 1

Year: 2006 05 04 03 02 01 00

ISBN 0-88489-649-8

Genuine recycled paper with 10% post-consumer waste.
Printed with soy-based ink.

Contents

Foreword:
The Great Conversation

F OR PRAYER to become personal and transforming, there must be a *Thou* whom we can address. There must be an interactive Presence who listens, receives, cares, and releases us. Prayer cannot be about merely announcing, projecting, or ventilating, unless those sentiments are being given to Someone and received by Someone. This is the simplicity, the embarrassment, and the transforming character of biblical prayer. It is almost too much for postmodern people.

As a result we have regressed into a politically correct litany of needs that we call praying. Such prayer avoids the second-person addressee, relying on mere third-person "this is the case" or "this is the need" language—in the hope that now everyone has heard my concerns and maybe they will do something about it, or with the attitude that if someone is up there listening, it won't hurt to tell Her or Him about it. What has been lost is the dynamism, daring personalism, and profound connectedness that characterizes the prayers of the saints and prophets. The energy of faith is gone. Such prayer transforms no one, and perhaps bores God. It surely bores me when there is almost no difference between the prayer of the faithful at Mass and the announcements after Mass. What have we lost?

More than anything else, more valuable than anything else, is the experience of ourselves being addressed as a *Thou!* Until and unless we experience such interior certainty, we will probably not address Anyone in return. We will talk about God, we will notify God of things (in impersonal ways) almost as if to get them off our back, but we will not be involved in the great relationship of I and Thou that we call Christian prayer.

When we know the dignity and empowerment of being addressed, we become an I, a person, an "other" who is taken seriously, and we can now take ourselves seriously: "My God, this is not a game! It is for real. God is treating me as if I matter, as if God hears me and cares about me! Maybe I do matter. Maybe this whole thing called life *is* for real! Maybe I am for real! And, best of all, my wildest hopes and imaginings about God might also be real!" At that moment the universe rearranges itself, we are constellated differently in this world of things and beings, and quite simply, we are at home for the first time. An overused, and often poorly used, phrase for that experience is "being saved." You really can't do much better than that. It's as good as it gets!

When we dare to continue the dialogue and shout into the quickly disappearing darkness, we discover that we can continue the conversation. Our words are being received and returned in subtle but very substantial ways over time. We are not just an anonymous "I" to the addressee, who has become a tender "Thou." The circuit is complete, and the true spiritual journey can at last begin. One wonders—is there any other beginning place at all?

It is unfortunate that the English language does not make this movement as clear as other languages that have two readily used words for *you*—one *you* for impersonal, initial, and functional relatedness, and another *you* for when you have crossed a line of intimacy, authority, or respect. To overcome the limitations of our word *you,* we turned to the Old English word *Thou* to try to communicate intimacy and respect. It is interesting that the places we maintained this "Thou" language were the Scriptures, prayer forms, and liturgical music. Here we could not deny the intimacy, the safety, the at-homeness, the mutual vulnerability that true prayer always leads us toward.

Why would anyone want to give up this precious heritage? Why would Christians abandon such a universally desired experience for mere third-person notifications and clarifications? Why have we merely fought over third-person language instead of even more insisting on our right to say "Thou" and to hear "Thou"?

It will make little difference if God is She or He if we do not first learn how to enter into blessed conversation itself. (Which is not to deny the place and importance of gender issues and inclusive language.) But orthopraxy will almost always precede real orthodoxy. For some reason we think that if we get all the language "orthodox," correct practice and experience will necessarily follow. The progressive folks have often fallen into the same trap they criticize in the conservatives. The true traditionalists put it well: *Lex orandi est lex credendi,* how we actually pray or converse will determine how and what we finally believe. And the passion of intimate union with God will lead into a human world of safety and surrender.

Joseph Schmidt has given us an excellent method of orthopraxy here. There is no way to get lost in ideology, metaphysical wrangling, or rarefied discussions *about* prayer here. He roots and grounds prayer in the place of the Incarnation, he takes seriously what apparently God takes seriously—our lives, our experiences, our everyday world. This is biblical and Christian prayer at its best. This is true orthodoxy without even trying to be. This is the great conversation that transforms human lives and gives joy to God. It's hard to believe that we could make a difference to God, but that is precisely what one drawn into the Mystery knows for sure! All else is accidental.

Richard Rohr, OFM
Center for Action and Contemplation
Albuquerque, New Mexico
Feast of Saint Teresa of Ávila

Preface

Many of us sense that honest reflection on the ordinary experiences of our life has a prayer value. As we look over the times that have been occasions of spiritual growth for us, we realize that some of these times, perhaps even the majority, occurred when we took stock of ourselves and got in touch with the significance of an event in our life. It might have been the brief experience of a phone call from a friend at a time of grief, or the lengthy experience of years of discouragement and frustration. At the time, we might not have thought we were praying, but in retrospect we sense that all the elements of prayer were present: we felt the sinfulness of being ego-centered; we felt the graciousness of God's work in us; we felt, simply, the closeness of the Lord and the call to a deeper authenticity in our life. In this essay I will explore the implications of sincere reflection on our experience as a way of prayer, and I am calling this kind of reflection *praying our experiences*.

To begin with, I would like to make these observations:

1. By *experiences* I mean not only our sense awarenesses but also much more. The word *experiences* here includes not just happenings in their external aspects—the sight of a flower, the news of a war, the pain of an injury—but also who I am now as the person who has had this sensory awareness. Experiences, therefore, also include all the feelings, memories, and desires that are generated by the awareness.

2. By *praying* I mean offering in honesty and surrender the reality of myself and my life history to the Lord. This may sometimes take the form of a recited prayer formula, because some of these formulas may help to express my own feelings of longing to be in union with God. Often, however, praying our experiences will take the form of simple, direct, and very personal speaking to the Lord. Prayer formulas may not always appropriately and adequately convey the concrete content of the totally unique and private happenings of my life, nor can formulas always embody the personal feelings of joy or anger I wish to express to the Lord.

3. By *praying our experiences,* then, I mean more than daydreaming, more than reminiscing, more than planning, more than pouting over the past. I mean getting in touch with who I am as the person who has had an experience, and offering that *who* to God through reflection on that experience. However, I do not wish to exclude daydreaming, reminiscing, planning, or pouting as experiences that themselves could be made the content of a prayer offering, nor do I mean that we pray only our good or joyful experiences. What I am advocating is that we pray *all* our experiences.

4. Praying our experiences is, I believe, a way of prayer that is valid and traditional. It is only one of many ways, and for some people a preliminary way in the journey of prayerfulness, but it constantly recurs because it is such a fundamental way of praying. Although it could degenerate into self-centeredness (and fear of this might be the reason it is not often suggested or tried as a way

of prayer), this form of prayer can ultimately lead to a depth of self-knowledge that purges self-centeredness.

5. Finally, I believe that praying one's experiences is exceedingly common among people who, ironically, not understanding it to be prayer, condemn themselves for not praying.

Introduction:
To Know Ourselves As God Knows Us

I WAS ABSOLUTELY FLOORED by what he said. We've been drinking buddies for twenty years, and this guy usually jokes all the time. Then, out of the blue, he has to get serious and say: 'Hey, pal, that's not right.' It was just the way he said it, or it was just the way I heard it, but I was stunned."

"And then what?" the priest asked.

"Well, I just thought about it, that was all. I knew something had to be done, and that's why I came to confession."

What Larry had thought about were the business trips, and the drinking and then the one-night stands that were becoming a part of them. He had argued with himself that everyone did things like that. His wife and children didn't know, and no real harm was being done. But his friend's out-of-the-blue comment had jolted him to reconsider.

One afternoon as he was routinely driving along an interstate highway on the way to meet a client, the remark of his friend came back to him. He felt some inner resistance, but turned off the car radio and began to think. Instead of arguing with himself or trying to justify himself, he let the entire matter of the business trips and sexual encounters surface in his awareness. He remembered the pattern of his actions during those times; he recalled the anticipation, the dissatisfaction.

Even as his memory worked, he noticed the feelings of anxiety, fear, and embarrassment welling up in him. He noticed his rising desire to blame circumstances and his wife for what he was beginning to see as a personal weakness. He realized that he wanted to forget the whole thing, to decide firmly to start over and let the past be past. He even began to recall a prayer he had memorized as a child. Then he realized that he was really trying to get rid of the pain that was surging up in him as the reality of the truth of these "incidents," as he called them, became more and more clear.

The memory and feelings associated with the drinking and the one-night stands were painful, agonizingly painful. And he hated the pain. But he also knew that there was a truth to be found in it. He had had an inkling of that in the force of his friend's simple statement: "Hey, pal, that's not right."

Now as he drove the interstate, Larry let the pain come on him; he waited. He resisted turning on the radio or daydreaming. He just waited in the fear and pain. There was nothing dramatic, but there was a certain clarity, and then the thoughts came: What are you really looking for in these one-night stands? Who are you becoming by getting involved in this way? Where is God in this experience? And then he knew that the remark by his friend had really been God's way of giving him a stiff kick. That's when he decided to get some help.

A month or so later, Larry told his friend he had thought about "things" and that he had gone to confession and was seeing a counselor.

Larry never considered his reflections about these "incidents" during that routine automobile drive as prayer. Prayer for him was something you did in church, or at least with formulas you had memorized as a child, or at the very least with readings out of a prayer book or the New Testament. And in any case, when you prayed you selected a topic that included something pious to say to God. None of this applied to that time of thinking as he drove the interstate.

Each day after she got Eddie off to school, Sue had a habit of spending fifteen minutes sitting in the living room reading the Psalms from her Bible. She read consecutively and slowly. On any given day she would get through only one psalm or part of one. She especially liked the psalms of praise, which she used as the basis for her own feelings of praise to God for all the wonderful things that God had done for the chosen people.

On one such occasion, she suddenly realized that Eddie had left his lunch on the floor by the door. She knew she would have to drop it off at school later in the morning. That made her think of Eddie's spontaneous way of doing things, which sometimes got him into trouble (he had forgotten his lunch after putting it down to give her a big hug and kiss), and then she thought of how he always seemed to manage to get out of trouble because his bouncy spirit and enthusiasm moved people to help him (as she was about to do by dropping the lunch off at school).

She smiled as she now thought about the way Eddie and his father, Ted, would banter about baseball, and how delighted she was the time she was called on to be the home-plate umpire as the two of them dramatized how the catcher *should* have played the bunted ball in the third inning with runners on first and third. Feelings of joy and gratitude welled up within her as she thought of Eddie and Ted, and Tracy still asleep in the crib upstairs, and Tiger the cat, sitting on the windowsill nodding stoically to the robins on the lawn.

The Bible had fallen closed on her lap. The God of the Hebrew Scriptures, so loving and so worthy of praise, she now began to realize, was her God and the God of her family. It was not a matter of her being worthy or deserving; it was a matter of God's simple goodness and beneficence. She knew that, too.

Later when she dropped off the lunch at school, she thanked the principal for passing the lunch along to Eddie and then added a word of thanks to the principal for doing all she could to make certain the kids were getting a good education.

The next morning Sue opened the Psalms and tried to be a little more disciplined about her reading because she wasn't sure she had "prayed" for the full fifteen minutes the morning before. She thought the lunch incident may have distracted her.

Sometimes we have the impression, as Larry did, that prayer is something you do in church or at least with some book or formula, or at the very least when you are considering something about God. Sometimes we get the feeling, as Sue did, that if we are reading psalms or reciting our favorite prayers or meditating on a passage of the Gospels, then any other thoughts would surely be distractions. But if we take time to consider when we have been most prayerful, even if we don't know exactly how the word *prayerful* would be defined by the experts, we may be surprised to realize that in our own experience, prayerful times and times of prayer might not exactly coincide.

If we are in a group prayer service or participating in a liturgical service, then, of course, our commitment is to the community prayer as well as to our own private needs and reflections. And at such times our prayer will reflect that. But if we consider the times when we have been prayerful alone, we may realize that some times of prayer have not been very prayerful and that some times of prayerfulness have not been "official" times of prayer.

Larry might give the Holy Spirit a little more cooperation if he more frequently took time out to reflect on just what was happening in his life, as he did on the interstate after his friend's comment. Of course, Larry would say he was only "thinking," and he would be right, but from another point of view, what he was doing could also be described as praying his life experiences.

Larry was honestly searching for the truth in those "incidents" that were beginning to concern him. And in this search he did not allow himself to be too sidetracked by cheap excuses or to be intimidated by fear or embarrassment. He was searching for the truth, and any time we search for truth, we are really searching for God.

Jesus' self-identification as "the Truth" and his description of the Holy Spirit as the Spirit of Truth certainly should give us confidence that our search for truth in our life is itself a prayer.

It would also be accurate to say that we can strive to grasp the truth, or meaning, of our life only because we have already been grasped by the Truth. At our moments of struggling to cut through our self-deception, we are like Larry, experiencing what Saint Paul describes as the Holy Spirit praying within us in ways that we do not even know.

Many great saints have described experiences of prayer, and almost all of these descriptions imply that even during the rare moments of the most advanced prayer, there is always movement along this path of searching for and coming to the truth of who we are in the presence of God. Prayer is not a matter of formulas or pious thoughts, it is a matter of honesty and searching for the meaning, the Truth of our experiences, however painful that may be.

As Sue continues to read and reflect on the Psalms, she will notice that the Psalms themselves directly address God not only in praise and thanks but also in frustration and fear, hope and despair, vengefulness and joy and self-pity. In other words, the prayer form of the Psalms conveys all the questions and feelings that arise out of the life experiences of a people striving to understand the meaning and direction of their lives. Sue's praise and thanksgiving for her family and her life joins with the sentiments of the Psalms giving thanks to the Creator and Gift-giver of all.

When Sue noticed the forgotten lunch by the door, she was, of course, distracted from reading and thinking about the Psalms. But she was not distracted from prayer. During those moments of what she might call "distraction," she was actually understanding in a new way some significant experiences of her life. She was distracted from her customary prayer-time agenda, but she was continuing her prayer now in a way that was more personal, more incarnational, more rooted in who she was at that moment in the hands of a loving God. Sue's "distraction" could be described as a way of praying her experiences.

On that particular morning, Sue's prayer was predominantly one of joy and gratitude, because her "distractions" led her into memories of happy experiences. On another morning while reading the Psalms, her "distractions" may take her into thoughts about an argument she had with Ted the evening before. If she is not sidetracked by thoughts of self-pity or self-justification or plans to get even, but is truthful and open about the experience, asking God what this argument must say to her about herself and her relationship with Ted, and honestly seeking to become aware of what the argument providentially calls her to, then her communication with God may include anger and frustration, regret and repentance. And that will be prayer, too, because that will be an honest if painful step in the search for truth in her life.

In praying our experiences, what matters is not so much the particular sentiments that come to us or the pious quality of our thoughts, but our desire to be more and more open to the Truth revealed in the truth of our experiences.

To pray our experiences is not to pray to win or to succeed, or to obtain the things we think we need in order to be content and happy. It is not to pray for what is external to our deepest concerns. It is rather to pray for enlightenment and courage and acceptance and gratitude.

Praying our experiences is praying to know ourselves as God knows us in a particular experience of our life, to accept ourselves as God accepts us, to love ourselves and others as God loves us, and to act in a Christlike way in response to what we come to know to be God's call in that particular experience.

This form of prayer is not worrying or planning or aimlessly daydreaming. It is not devising a strategy or rationalizing about a memory. It is coming to know that we are held in God's infinite love and mercy as that all-encompassing truth is focused and revealed in a particular experience.

Our God is always with us. We come to know God in and through our daily life experiences because God is the source of our existence and God's mercy is the very heart of our life. We come to know God by knowing that our life is penetrated with God's knowledge and love, not only always and everywhere but also here and now in this particular experience.

This kind of prayer is always possible, but we may not always be attracted to it. Rather, we may be drawn to hear God's word through reflection on a passage of the Scriptures, or we may find ourselves called to be in simple attention to the presence of God. But at times we may also find ourselves praying our experiences, as did Sue and Larry. Then, hearing the word of God in the events of our daily life, we will be challenged and consoled, confirmed and confronted, judged and ultimately graced with the peace of knowing that the God of history and the universe is truly the God of the mundane experiences of our life as well.

Sue's and Larry's experiences have parallels in the Scriptures themselves. One such parallel is in Luke's story of the Annunciation.

Mary may have been at prayer, meditating on the Psalms or conversing with the Lord as she went about tidying up the house. But she was interrupted in her prayer by a sudden awareness, which Luke describes as the message of an angel: "Rejoice, O highly favored daughter. The Lord is with you. Blessed are you among women."

Mary was troubled and wondered what the greeting meant. "Do not fear, Mary," the angel said, "You have found favor with God. You shall conceive and bear a son and give him the name Jesus."

Now Mary's disturbance was deep indeed. Feelings of anxiety and fear were aroused in her. How, she wondered, could this be? Her awareness of God's presence and the inkling of what was being asked of her challenged deep areas of her self-identity. Who was she, to be so favored by God, to be asked to involve herself in such a way in the work of salvation?

"I do not know man." Now thoughts of her family, of her decision to marry Joseph, feelings of confusion and fear all must have surged up in Mary. What does the Lord want? What am I called to do? How can this be possible? But Mary was open to her Lord; she wanted to hear the truth; she desired so much to accept the will of her God. What could all this mean?

Perhaps Mary's reflections and struggle lasted for a few minutes or a few hours; perhaps they continued for a few days or many weeks. Luke telescopes the scene into a continuing dialogue, and says the angel answered Mary: "The Holy Spirit will come upon you and the power of the most High will overshadow you. . . . Nothing is impossible with God."

And now Mary knew that she was being called on to be filled with the Holy Spirit, to be possessed by the power of God in her life. She was being asked to give up the subtle resistance raised by her self-image, her personal plans, her previous decisions, her own agenda in life.

She prayed this experience with all its memories and all its feelings of confusion and fear, of joy and surrender. She did not dismiss the angel's announcement as an intrusion into her daily prayer schedule. Rather, struggling to come to the truth of her life in the presence of God, her conversing with the angel became her prayer.

Luke's story of the Annunciation is the story of Christian prayer. Mary opened her heart to her God by hearing and responding to God's call. Her prayer was to search for truth, for meaning in her life, and through the overshadowing of the Spirit of Truth, she was the first to receive him who would call himself the Truth.

A common element in the prayer of Mary, Larry, and Sue is that each in his or her own unique way allowed the Spirit of Truth to bring a new and truth-filled illumination to the experiences of life. To receive this truth, each had to avoid indulging in the preoccupation of the moment or being sidetracked by feelings of fear or self-pity, self-satisfaction or self-aggrandizement. Each accepted the new awareness and responded with honesty.

For Sue this meant being more conscious of the gifts in her own life and cultivating a sense of gratefulness that began to include all of life. For Larry it meant being aware of a personal weakness and opening himself to union with God through repentance. For Mary it meant accepting a new self-identity and an openness to a completely unexpected future. For all three it meant being grasped by the Spirit of Truth and saying yes to that loving embrace.

1. Beginning to Pray Our Experiences:
Notions of Prayer

PRAYING OUR EXPERIENCES is the practice of reflecting on and entering honestly into our everyday experiences in order to become aware of God's word in them and to offer ourselves through them to God. We are getting in touch with who we are as people who have had personal experiences and are offering our whole self to God through reflection on the events in our life.

We pray our experiences when we use the content of our lived existence as the content of our prayer. Our memories and desires evoke the concrete happenings of our past as well as our plans and hopes for the future. These feelings and memories are the very focus of our prayer when we pray our experiences.

All of us have probably prayed this way, although we called it by another name. We called it "just thinking" when, on a sickbed, we spent restless and empty days pondering. We called it "questioning" when, after an experience of failure and despair, we passed sleepless nights asking "why?" We called it "resting" when we did nothing of consequence as we vacationed after a particularly stressful period. Yet, in retrospect, this time of thinking, questioning, and getting ourselves together might have been as helpful to our faith life as hours of formal prayer. We had indeed been praying our experiences, unfolding our memories and feelings in the presence of the Lord to see what our day-to-day living might be telling us and to what it might be calling us.

We might have been invited to such prayer, for example, by the chance word of a friend. We might have been taken aback by that word because it aroused in us feelings and memories out of proportion to its importance. We wonder at the power that the offhand remark had over us, and we are drawn not just to react to the intention or literal meaning of the speaker, but to enter into the significance of the sentiments and memories awakened in us.

A remark by an acquaintance may illumine part of ourselves that we had not seen so clearly before. Consider the following illustration: We are planning to make a retreat at a certain spiritual center, which has been the site of so many graces before. We tell an acquaintance about our plans, and the person comments offhandedly, "Oh, you want to be consoled by your friends again." The remark has power. We try to ignore it, but it does not go away. We reflect on this experience and recognize our need for the attention of others. The consolation and affection lavished by friends are more important to us than the quiet and solitude of the retreat setting. We may also sense a desire to be thought pious. Our wish to be closer to God is present, too, of course, but reflecting more on our deep response to the chance remark reveals with great clarity the ambiguity of our intention. We begin to unfold the implications of all this: what it says about our weaknesses and our strengths, what it says about past retreats, what it says about our relationships with those at the spiritual center we call friends, and what it says about our response to God's call. Thus, the remarks of others—whether complimentary, sarcastic, or merely offhanded—can be invitations to pray our experiences.

Further, our understanding of what prayer should be makes us uneasy when our own memories and feelings intrude during a time of prayer. Sometimes we take specific measures to block out memories and feelings, believing that details of our life are not the proper content of prayer. We might have been taught that prayer is an activity quite sublime and otherworldly. We probably learned that in prayer we should talk to God about God. So we may consider prayer to involve some kind of mental image of God and to be focused on some kind of spiritual center outside of ourselves. Consequently, we ordinarily regard reflection on our experiences as an obstacle because it roots us to ourselves and prevents our flight to the desired level of communion with God. This, I believe, is a common but narrow way of viewing prayer.

We have been taught that only as a kind of last resort can our ordinary concerns and experiences be appropriate in prayer. Thus, if the memory of a friend arises during prayer, we might say a brief prayer for the person, but we then return to our "proper" praying. If the memory of a moment of jealousy or pride comes to mind during prayer, if the remembrance of a childhood event or feelings of hurt and rejection fill us, we try to rid ourselves of these distractions and move back to our formal praying. We may even baptize our distractions with a brief moment of prayer if we cannot rid ourselves of them immediately.

Without being fully aware of all the implications, we might have simply defined memories and feelings out of our prayer. We might have named them distractions because we have decided that our prayer for today or for this week will be such and so, and these memories are therefore uncalled for. What I am suggesting, however, is to make these very distractions the content of our prayer—but not in order to solve problems, not to forward our projects, not to worry, not to plan, not to lick our wounds in self-pity. Rather, we focus on our experiences in order to get in touch with their revelatory power. We hear God's word in them, and we are called to respond.

Praying our experiences is a form of prayer that can be particularly helpful at the end of a busy day. As we come to prayer at that time, our mind is filled with memories of projects and human encounters. We find ourselves flooded by the pleasant or humiliating feelings that arise from the memories of our behavior. If at this time we try to meditate on one of the mysteries in the life of Jesus, or open ourselves simply to the Lord's presence in imageless prayer, we soon find ourselves in an impossible struggle. We recall the harsh word we said so sarcastically during the day. We recall our hurt pride at an admonition or our anger at not being notified of a schedule change. Or we recall our joy at the phone call from a friend visiting town or the kindness and patience we extended to a stranger.

If we look upon these recollections as distractions to our prayer, then we will be constantly fighting them, and we may consider our prayer time to be a waste. But if we accept them as an integral part of our prayer, then our prayer can take on new aspects and power. We begin to know more clearly both the integrity and the brokenness of our motivation; we can sense more realistically our duplicity; we can become more aware of our goodness; we can see more sharply our values and priorities.

During this type of prayer, we might not generate pious thoughts. We might not read the Scriptures. We might not use theological language in our reflection. We may not feel we are resting in the Lord. But in sensing the peace and the call that we know are the signs of yielding to God's presence in our life, we know we are praying.

Praying our experiences means being open to seeing ourselves as we are and to seeing our personal history— as it is known to the Lord. This requires an awareness and an honesty that will root us in our actual daily life. It will lead us to talk to God about ourselves because we are in God's hands, and it will challenge us to growth through purifying self-knowledge. In other words, we will recognize the Divine within ourselves rather than engage in some sublime and otherworldly activity of imagining a God out there.

Another impression we sometimes have about prayer is that because we pray for the sake of God's glory, we need not be overly concerned if our prayer does not produce any transformation in ourselves. We try to explain away the fact that our prayer is often ineffective in renewing our daily life. Moreover, it seems contrived that various kinds of meditation require that we form a resolution to be carried out during the day for the sake of self-improvement. Praying our experiences, on the other hand, directly addresses the uneasiness we feel at the number of hours we have spent in formal prayer and the small effect these have had on our way of thinking and acting in daily life. In the process of praying our experiences, we resolve this dichotomy between our longing to glorify God and the process of our own transformation. When we pray our experiences, we need not apply the meditation to ourselves; the meditation is about ourselves as we hold ourselves before the Lord in an offering of humility and resignation. Here, in our self-knowledge, we find the content of our praise, our thanksgiving, and our offering to God.

2. Self-Knowledge:
Giftedness and Brokenness

Saint Teresa of Ávila made a significant comment about reflection on experiences and personal history. In her autobiography, Teresa tried to balance the need to go beyond self-knowledge in prayer with the continual need to return to it. She said:

> This path of self knowledge must never be abandoned, nor is there on this journey a soul so much a giant that it has no need to return often to the stage of an infant and a suckling. And this should never be forgotten. . . . There is no stage of prayer so sublime that it isn't necessary to return often to the beginning. Along this path of prayer, self knowledge and the thought of one's sins is the bread with which all palates must be fed no matter how delicate they may be; they cannot be sustained without this bread.

Here Teresa insists that we must never close off the path of self-knowledge as a path of prayer. Consideration of heavenly things, the imaging of the Totally Other, or reflection on one of the mysteries of Jesus' life are all important ways into prayer, as is the elimination of all images in the total quiet of the Lord's presence. However, if we believe that these are the *only* paths of prayer, the thoughts of our own experiences will naturally appear to be distractions. Teresa's emphasis on the "bread" of self-knowledge can help us to an expanded understanding of what prayer might be.

The Lord, as we know, wants the offering of ourselves. We sometimes fail to see, however, that this offering is not made in some abstract way with pious words or readings but is rooted in the acceptance of the concrete details of our life. The offering of ourselves can only be the offering of our lived experience because this alone is ourselves. In our prayer we take ourselves into our hands and offer to God our whole self—our strengths and our weaknesses. As Teresa said so simply, "This path of self knowledge must never be abandoned."

Another reason we must never abandon the path of self-knowledge is that authentic self-knowledge is not knowledge about our superficial ego. It is knowledge about our true self, and therefore it is knowledge about ourselves in relationship to humankind, to all of creation, and ultimately to God.

When we speak of authentic self-knowledge, we are referring to the awareness of ourselves as we are in God's eyes. There is, therefore, no depth of self-knowledge without a depth of faith. Within this context of faith, self-knowledge grows and is understood as we become more aware of both our giftedness and our brokenness. Each of these aspects speaks not only of ourselves but also of God as God relates to us.

Our giftedness speaks to us of God's goodness because in our giftedness we come to know we have nothing that we have not received. In the context of faith, the gifts of our talents, health, and friendships cry out to us of God. If a person believes that the love of a friend is merited, or that purity of motivation is the result of careful planning, that person is probably someone with superficial self-knowledge. These are gifts, pure and simple. It is far from the truth to believe that personal holiness can result from proper management of life details or that trust in God is the fruit of personal strategy and effort. To the extent we have grown in faith and trust, to that extent we have been gifted. No amount of our own cleverness has produced it. As we grow in self-knowledge, we begin to experience God's beneficence—until we at last realize that *all* of life is a gift.

We may also receive genuine appreciation from the people with whom we live and work. They may say a word of thanks for the good we have done to them by our counsel, or they may tell us how much our friendship has meant to them. We acknowledge the good in ourselves, yet often we are embarrassed. We feel that our efforts have not been great enough to warrant such gratitude. We know that our motivation has been tinged with selfishness. In praying these experiences, we become aware that the power going out from us to effect good in others originates well beyond ourselves. We begin to appreciate the power of the Spirit we now sense operating through us. Our patience, our gentleness, our understanding—all have been used by the God beyond us. The goodness of the Spirit has used our goodness, and we feel ourselves drawn to offer thanks to God for both.

The awareness of our sinfulness or brokenness also speaks to us of God, for, paradoxically, our sinfulness is also a gift. In referring to self-knowledge as a path of prayer, Teresa said, "The thought of one's sins is the bread with which all palates must be fed." Our duplicity, our lust, our narcissism, our sloth—all speak to us of the fundamental brokenness in our life. We know that no matter what our cleverness or strategies are in the face of this brokenness, we cannot rid ourselves of one speck of duplicity or one scintilla of narcissism. Sometimes we are frightened by the depth of our evil, and we try to ignore it. Yet, in paradox, our sinfulness becomes our bread. In a mysterious way, we can be nourished by our own evil if we accept that evil as part of the truth about ourselves and offer that truth to the Lord.

Saint Paul spoke of glorying in his weaknesses. He had reached a depth of self-knowledge that permitted him to understand that his righteousness consisted not in freedom from weakness and sin but in being able to say yes to his entire life and his whole self. Paul knew that although a yes to life meant a yes to his own evil, it was also a yes to the God who in the evil was sustaining him in love and drawing him to good. For Paul the path of faith, not the way of works, was the right path to God because he knew goodness is a gift of God, not something we can achieve by our own cleverness or effort.

Paul had the boldness to acknowledge that he had in the past, and would continue in the future, done the things that he did not want to do. He knew he was a sinful person, one who would never reach that chimerical perfection of being faultless. He sought, rather, that Christian holiness of being integral, of accepting into his offering to God his strengths and his weaknesses, his virtues and his sins. Paul offered his total self to God, not only what he would like to be, but what in truth he was. Offering ourselves in truth is the offering that God asks and that forms the basis of prayer.

In one of her letters, Thérèse of Lisieux revealed that she shared Paul's insight. "You are wrong," she wrote,

> if you think your little Thérèse always marches with ardour along the way of virtue, she is weak, very weak; every day she experiences it afresh; but . . . Jesus delights to teach her, as He taught St. Paul, the science of glorying in one's infirmities; that is a great grace, and I beg Jesus to teach it to you, for in it alone is found peace and rest for the heart. Seeing yourself so worthless, you wish no longer to look at yourself, you look only at the sole Beloved!

Thérèse used this awareness as the basis of her "little Way." "Perfection seems easy to me," she remarked. "I realize that it is sufficient that we acknowledge our nothingness and abandon ourselves like a child into the arms of our good Lord."

In our brokenness we come to know God's acceptance and love. In the depths of our heart, we sense God's spirit acting toward healing and integration. That self-knowledge leads us to an awareness of both our evil and God's strength, an awareness that goes beyond what we could know from any theological formula. Thérèse acknowledged, "No book, no theologian taught [this Way] to me, and yet I feel in the depths of my heart that I possess the truth." We come to a knowledge similar to that which Paul, Mary Magdalene, and Peter had of Jesus and his way with sinners. In faith, self-knowledge leads us to a self-acceptance and a self-love that reach into an awareness of God's love.

Praying our experiences is a way into this depth of self-knowledge and acceptance. As we unfold our experiences and become aware of our blessedness and our brokenness, we begin to become more aware of the God who alone can fill all of our life with graciousness.

3. Introspection:
Narcissism and the Limited Ego

IN THE SEARCH OF OUR EXPERIENCES, in the unfolding of
memories to learn of our weaknesses and giftedness,
are we not in danger of focusing on ourselves in a
narcissistic way? Are we not in the further danger of
rationalizing and manipulating our experiences so they
tell us what we want to hear?

These dangers are, of course, present; but they are
dangers on the right road. We must move with some
caution but not turn back.

How can we, in this unfolding of experiences, avoid
the dangers of narcissistic daydreaming on the one hand
and rationalizing or even denying our memories on the
other? When egoism and rationalization are already
our primary approaches in life, these dangers are quite
real—it becomes difficult to avoid narcissism in *anything*
we do, even in prayer. But if our life is being lived with
reverence and purity of heart, then reflecting on our
experiences will be steeped in this same reverence and
purity. The life-stance with which we approach reflection, rather than the reflection itself, is crucial.

In this regard we may remember being warned against
loving ourselves, lest we fall into a form of selfishness.
Now we have come to realize that loving ourselves is
not at all selfish and that if we do not love ourselves
we are seriously weakened in our human and spiritual
growth. Loving ourselves is important in our full development and is the foundation of our love of others.

In the same way, seeing reflection on our personal history as an obstacle to raising our mind and heart to God is a myopic view. Authentic reflection on life, like authentic love of self, is not the problem but part of the solution.

The very exercise of open and honest reflection will, in fact, help us to discern the extent to which selfishness and rationalization control our life-stance. It is a clue that we are indulging in unhealthy introspection when we find our ego is the source of energy and our small world is closing in on us. We then find ourselves judging the memory of our experiences in terms of our ego expectations and hopes, and events of our life are labeled good or bad according to our own standards or those imposed on us. We find ourselves congratulating or reprimanding ourselves depending on whether we have appeared wise or foolish, powerful or weak, clever or obtuse, good or bad. Our reflections are not so much on what our experiences are saying to us as on what we assess to be their value in enhancing our stature as successful persons or in crushing us as failures.

Narcissism makes our ego the center of our world and leads us away from honesty with ourselves. Narcissism prevents us from being receptive to the truth of our experiences. We close in on ourselves, not because reflection is dangerous, but because our stance is one of egocentrism. When we find ourselves not listening to our total experience but excluding part of it, or evaluating it according to our own expectations, then we can begin to suspect a narcissistic stance. When we dissect rather than receive, when we make our reflections ethical considerations of what should be rather than faith-awareness of what is, or when we manipulate our reflections by refusing to enter certain areas of our life, even areas of religious piety and devotion, then to that extent we have placed conditions on our finding God's word in our experiences.

We may also stifle the voice of our experience by controlling our memory and feelings with a refined rationalism. We rein in our imagination and muzzle our feelings. Can anything good come out of Nazareth? we ask, and we do not go to see. Our rational and analytic thought process becomes a barrier and leaves no crack for the unexpected inspiration or the surprise awareness. We have domesticated God, and our experiences cannot speak truth to us.

In this way we may be like the Pharisees who imposed their rationalism, their egos, and their Law on their experience of Jesus. Jesus' words of forgiveness and acts of healing were not seen as manifestations of God's power because Jesus' acts did not square with the Pharisees' analytic preconceptions:

- If he were the Messiah, he would know what kind of woman she is who is washing his feet.
- The Messiah would not do such and so because we know what the Savior will and will not do.

The natural feelings of sympathy and admiration that the Pharisees must have had for Jesus were stifled by their preconceptions. They left no room for the unexpected in their experience, and so an awareness of God could not enter.

The Eastern mystical tradition is perhaps more conscious of this difficulty with preconceptions than is the Western popular spirituality. In some forms of Eastern discipline, in order to open the disciple's mind to the nonrational and to the unexpected, the religious master presents the spiritual novice with a *koan* as the focus for meditation. The koan is a statement or question that makes no sense. It usually includes elements that offer no coherent or reasonable basis from which an analysis can be made. The classic koan "What is the sound of one hand clapping?" contains elements that are themselves in contradiction, and so no reasonable answer by analysis is possible. This is the point. In meditating on the koan, the novice, perhaps after months or years, comes to an awareness that rational analysis will not do; the answer, if there be an answer, must come from beyond rationality and analysis, which is to say, from beyond the ego.

The understanding of the koan does not come from rationalizing or manipulating the data but emerges in the ego's act of yielding to helplessness. Therefore, it is not a matter of rationally working at the koan that brings awareness. Rather, being in *faith* with the koan leads to personal awareness and transformation.

In a similar way, we might say that many of our experiences are themselves koans. They contain elements that we see as contradictory and as making no sense: the death of a beloved child, failure in an area of special competence, a serious injury, falling in love. We ask ourselves for an answer or a meaning. We analyze and reason, but no understanding is forthcoming. Again, that is the point.

It is not by rational analysis or by the manipulation of the data of our experience that the answer will come but by an egoless reflection in which we open ourselves to a source of power beyond ourselves. It is not by rationally working at the memory of our experiences that we gain awareness; rather, by being in faith with our experiences, we grow to a sense of our finiteness and giftedness, and therefore to a sense of God's power and care. Reflecting on our experiences in a reverent way, far from being narcissistic, opens us to the source of life on the other side of our limited rational ego.

4. Healing the Past:
Naming, Accepting, and Forgiving

ALL OUR EXPERIENCES possess a revelatory power, yet we find ourselves unable to reflect on some of them. They are too disconcerting. They are too hurtful. We do not want to feel again the pain of the argument with a friend, which ruptured a budding and precious relationship. We do not want ever again to feel the sense of rejection and loneliness that the memory of our relationship with our father or mother may bring. We resist reminders of our jealousy or our sensuality that have led us into spiteful and selfish acts. We do not want to think about our failure as a young teacher or our blunders in our first years of marriage. We do not want to reflect on how badly we handle human relationships and how slothful we are. We do not want to reopen wounds that have scarred over.

When we label these painful experiences *wounds,* we must remember that this is *our* label. We say they are injuries to our sensitivities, to our expectations, to our hopes, to our sense of propriety and dignity and success; but as they manifest a part of the truth about ourselves, they are not wounds but facets of the precious totality of our life. Our prayer will be hindered to the extent that we cannot gather up all of the reality of our life into our offering to God.

Prayer is fundamentally an offering of ourselves to God. It is not a matter of offering the pious thoughts of theologians or spiritual writers. Nor is it a matter of offering to God only what we believe to be worthy of the Creator—our successes, our virtues, our goodness—as if they were our achievements to be given with a dignified obeisance. We offer to God who we are now: all of those longings for the Lord and all of those egotistical schemes that form part of our desires. All of this is part of us, and this is all we have to offer to God.

The parts of ourselves left out of our offering weaken our gift. God wants all of us, and so we work toward an integration of all of our memories and hopes into our total gift. To achieve this integrity requires that in some way the memories that cause pain and resistance must be healed.

When we refer to the healing of memories, we are not speaking about morbidly dragging up hurtful experiences that have already settled. We are speaking of those painful experiences that are still with us and cry out for our attention. These memories come to us often by surprise. They recur when we least expect them. We do not drag them up; they come to our awareness of their own power, so to speak, because they have more to say to us. They are the memories that, like festering wounds, tell us they need attention.

In acknowledging our painful experiences as part of our personal history, we begin to open ourselves to the possibility of being nourished by God through those experiences. To the extent that we deny an experience, however hurtful, we deny God's loving care, which is mysteriously embedded in that experience.

Sometimes we may fear that if we even acknowledge a painful experience, it will gain control over us. We falsely imagine that if we simply never think of it again, it will go away. This, of course, does not happen.

On the one hand, if an experience causes pain and disturbance when it comes to mind, we can be certain that it is disturbing us even when we are not aware of it. Casting an experience out of our memory does not cast its power out of our life. By not acknowledging and accepting these painful memories, we permit them to have power over us. We become bound by that part of our past. We are not free in relationship to it. We are defensive toward it, and we cannot be nourished by it.

On the other hand, this lack of freedom is also an indication of a blockage in our prayer. We have not yet gathered together all of ourselves in our offering to the Lord.

Rejecting the past as something "I'll never think of again" does not free us, but rather we free ourselves when we integrate our past into our total life history, so that our past and ourselves become one. The offering of ourselves to the Lord, then, approaches a completeness.

By ignoring painful experiences, we allow them to control us in a profound and subtle way. By acknowledging them, we begin to reduce their control and begin to gain power over them. A helpful example of this is the notion of "naming" in the Scriptures. God required Adam to name the animals before Adam could have dominion over them. This was a sign that Adam's rela-

tionship to the animals was one of freedom and power.
When Jesus wished to manifest lordship over Peter, Jesus
named Peter. For us, too, naming an experience gives us
dominion over it, not by crushing it, but by integrating
it into our life as Adam accepted the animals into his
world and as Jesus accepted Peter as a leader in the
church.

In acknowledging a painful experience, we begin
the process of healing because we begin the process of
living the truth. This truth, Jesus assures us, will set us
free because it is enfolded in that most ultimate of truths:
God's love. The process of healing of memories is primarily a process of letting the whole truth of our personal
history be enfolded in the all-encompassing truth of
God's love.

By our simple acknowledgment, we take the first
step toward healing the pain of the memory. The second
step is to broaden that acknowledgment into the feeling
of acceptance, admitting both the experience and the
pain as a part of ourselves.

At this point not only have we recognized that a
painful experience does exist in our life, but we have
begun to accept it as a significant one. We now begin to
realize that by its recurrence in memory and by the intensity of the related pain, the experience is asking to be
brought to a reconciliation. This reconciliation begins
when our relationship with the event shifts from that
of an adversarial (over-against) relationship to that of a
dialogical (one-with) relationship. This shift indicates that

we have come to a level of reverence and respect for the experience, realizing that it may speak truth to us. Prayer has often been described as listening to God; we may hear God if we open ourselves to hear what our painful experience has to say.

Our personal life will speak to us when we allow open quiet to follow our questions:

- What does this experience have to say about my way of living, my way of relating to others?
- What does this experience have to say about my priorities in life?
- What is the cause of the hurt?
- What would it require for the experience to no longer hurt?
- What does all of this say about my ability to abandon myself "like a child into the arms of our good Lord"?

Further, moving from acknowledging a painful experience to accepting it with reverence often calls for forgiveness. Frequently the pain itself is rooted in the need to forgive: we have not forgiven ourselves, and we have not forgiven others.

Perhaps the painful experience showed us our weakness or sinfulness. Perhaps our stupidity or sloth or self-centeredness motivated us to a foolish action we now sincerely regret. The memory brings with it a deep awareness of the sinfulness that is still with us. At times we cannot believe the Lord has already forgiven us, and we forget that Jesus asks us to forgive ourselves.

Perhaps the painful experience was caused by the cruelty of others or by their insensitivity or their hatred toward us. Whether the problem lasted several minutes or several years, we are now called to forgive the other and to move our attention from the hurt to the Lord. We are asked to accept the reality that the Lord who loves both us and the other is offering us this memory as a way of getting closer to Jesus.

Forgiveness of ourselves and others does not require a rational justification; indeed it often will not bear one. But forgiveness does require faith in the power of the Lord's love to bring good out of evil. This faith will not be achieved merely by our rethinking the experience. Our reason fails because God's forgiveness and power are not encompassed by reason. Rather our faith is kindled in the quiet of imaging the Lord moving toward us, accepting us and others as Jesus accepted Zacchaeus and the adulterous woman. In our imagination we can experience what our reason fails to comprehend. Abandoning and going beyond reason, we can experience the warmth of the arms of our good Lord.

Forgiveness of ourselves and others allows us to accept more fully the memory of the experience as a part of ourselves. We can now more completely incorporate the event as a part of our offering to the Lord. We now also begin to realize that the painful experience is a source of growth because it invites us to accept both our sinfulness and God's love.

The final step in the healing of memories that follows from acknowledgment and acceptance is appreciation. Memories are healed and our prayer is complete when we come full cycle and appreciate our painful experience. We reverently take up that hard rock of experience rejected by the builders within ourselves and accept it as the cornerstone of a new stage of growth.

We say yes, a grateful yes, to all that has been. We embrace our experience as a little death leading to a little resurrection. Redemptive suffering is most likely to be found not in the suffering of the body or in some romanticized oppression, but in the profound sadness of realizing our pettiness and self-pity and absolute poverty before God. Thérèse remarked, "To suffer our imperfections with patience, this is true sanctity." This is also the awareness of Saint Paul when he prayed, "If I have to boast, I will boast of all the ways in which I am weak" (2 Corinthians 11:30).

- By the healing of memories we mean accepting our experiences with all the associated pain, realizing that all things work together unto good for those who love God.
- By the healing of memories we mean offering these experiences to God as our prayerful participation in the paschal mystery, in which death is swallowed up in victory.
- By the healing of memories we mean accepting into the treasury of self-giving to the Lord all of our experiences, especially those that have spoken to us so vividly of our vulnerability and sinfulness.

We know a memory has been healed when it speaks to us no longer of pain or brokenness but of God's mercy and love. The memory has been healed when we can say what Saint Thérèse said about the pain that her faults caused her: "The memory of my faults humbles me; it causes me never to rely on my own strength, which is but weakness, but especially it teaches me a further lesson of the mercy and love of God."

When we pray our experiences, we struggle to acknowledge, accept, forgive, integrate, and appreciate all of our personal history so that our prayer of offering might be complete. In the process we heal our memories because now those painful memories speak to us more of God's love than of our hurt.

5. Writing:
Discovery and Dialogue

A RE WE NOT TRAPPED in the cycle of trying to purify our reflective stance by means of the same process of reflection? A step out of this dilemma is also a step toward addressing the previously mentioned danger of allowing reflection to be dominated by the ego, narcissistic daydreaming, or aimless reminiscing. This step is the process of writing out our reflections.

The writing of reflections helps us become more conscious of the full dimensions of our experience. It also helps us become more aware of the degree of our narcissism by allowing us to note more objectively where the center of our concerns lies. We cannot write of our experiences for any length of time or in any depth without noting what so clearly lies on the paper before us. Recurring judgments, values, and hopes as well as descriptions of what we take to be our accomplishments and failures speak to us of our primary life-stance. In our writing, our narcissism will surely manifest itself—as will our search for the deeper truth of our life.

At the same time, writing helps us to stop spinning the wheels of our anxiety and prevents us from jumping aboard the merry-go-round of our egotistical daydreaming. If we merely *think* of our experiences without writing some or all of them on paper, we sometimes find our reflection diffused, scattered, or diverted. We might also find ourselves rethinking the same question a hundred times.

If we are anxious or disturbed about the significance of an experience, the memory tends to return, mushrooming in confusion with each repetition. We begin to feel overwhelmed and disoriented. The experience quickly assumes unmanageable proportions, contaminating other memories. Writing, however, has the power to focus and locate experiences so that they can be put into perspective within our total life and faith context. Juxtaposed in written form, experiences can be viewed in sequence, pattern, and proportion.

Writing our reflections also gives us an opportunity to move forward at our own pace in the exploration of painful experiences; it allows us simply to list memories and feelings too difficult to be written or meditated on fully. We may sense that these memories and feelings have a deeper message for us, but they may still be too hurtful to unfold. Our feelings of jealousy or sexuality may be too embarrassing to explore, for example, or the memory of our acts of deceit and sloth too unsettling to consider fully. Even merely listed, the jottings of these experiences and feelings remain as testimonies to our weakness and to our courage. We become aware of our fear and the power that the feelings and memories have over us, but at the same time we sense a message and know we will return sometime later to accept it more fully. Having simply named the experience, we know we can move on. In this way writing helps us in the process of the healing of memories, which we saw to be so essential for the offering of ourselves to God.

Further, writing helps us to open out those experiences and to search through those memories with which we are not immediately comfortable. We begin to see more clearly the patterns of choice leading into the experiences and the motivations and attitudes undergirding them. Gradually we become aware of precisely those elements of sinfulness and giftedness in our personal history in which we can especially recognize God's call.

Writing, however, may manifest its greatest power because of its creative and self-generating force. We do not merely put onto paper predetermined words and completed thoughts. Writing has the dynamic character of a movement into the unknown. It cannot fully be precontrolled by our intellect, and therefore we can never be sure of what the writing might yield. When we take pen in hand, we grasp a door handle and begin to open areas of our life history and present awareness that are deeper than we had imagined.

We write more than we are fully conscious of. We may write beyond what we had anticipated and over the edge of our intellectual awareness. Under our pen emerge reflections and insights and awarenesses that we have not articulated before, but which we have always known to be true at a prereflective level.

When we have finished writing, or when we reread our writing months later, we may say a surprised but honest yes to what we have written. We apparently know much more than we can put into our conscious and orderly thought, and these preconscious understandings emerge as we write and later reread. In writing over the edge of our conscious insights, we often reach a level of awareness that we know to be a gift of God. What opens to us in self-knowledge we know to be beyond what we could have called forth by our own power.

In writing reflections on our experience, we may also find that we are moved to engage in a kind of conversation. We find ourselves addressing the Lord directly in words of contrition and hope: "Lord, I want you; I need you. I am sorry for my wrongdoing; lead me."

And we find ourselves writing a reply as from the lips of the Lord: "Why are you afraid? Trust me."

Our conversation continues: "I fear giving in, Lord. I fear my deceit, my pride. I want to trust but cannot."

"You know you can trust; I am with you."

"But I am afraid, Lord; I am afraid to go too far. I want to control my life. I want to organize it."

"Don't you think I can see the deepest desires of your heart?"

"I want you, Lord, to be all in my life, but I hold back."

"You don't have to do everything. I am with you."

As our conversation continues, we are startled by the truths that unfold. Significance and awareness reach a clarity that we had not realized consciously before. We see ourselves in a new light, perhaps in a way we had known in our heart but which we could not articulate before. Conversing with the Lord puts us in touch with depths in our experience that we know to be true in the *world of the Lord* but which only now rise to conscious awareness. This insight often brings with it great consolation as we see our life in the hands of the Lord. On the other hand, it may also bring a sense of confrontation as we become aware of the force of our own duplicity. In recognizing here, often vividly, the blessedness of our life as well as the enormity of our own evil, we experience God's love and God's call.

Prior to our reflection, we might have judged an experience good or bad, a success or a failure, extraordinary or common; but now labels are no longer significant. We are aware that by judging an experience we have classified its importance and therefore controlled its impact. In the process of labeling, we have surrendered to the analysis of the ego and have manipulated our experience.

Bad and ordinary experiences, by their very classification, lose meaning and are relegated to marginal consideration. Yet the Scriptures speak of a *felix culpa*. Paul referred to glorying in bad experiences, and the Gospel speaks of the signs of the Kingdom in the most ordinary happenings. Although some events in our life may have more immediate impact than others, and some may make us appear more successful than others, what is important is the realization that *every* experience has a religious dimension. At root, every experience embodies the challenge God offers us in love to become more integral and Christlike.

Some may ask at this point whether the process of exploring our feelings and experiences in reflection and writing is prayer in the proper theological sense. Isn't prayer directed to God alone? Isn't it more properly thought of as a dialogue with the Totally Other?

We can approach an answer to these questions by taking seriously what we accept in faith to be certain. Nothing is more a gift from the Totally Other than our creation, our life, and our continued existence in God's love. As a gift, our life unfolds under God's loving care. God continually sustains us, graces us, and calls us. Each of our days is a gift and a call from the Creator. To reflect on our experiences, then, is to unwrap the gift, to listen to the call. Far from being a narcissistic activity, this reflection can be a way of centering on God, a way of hearing God's word addressed to us as individuals in the uniqueness of our person. It can be a way of taking seriously our faith in God's providence and our belief that all is grace.

The words of Thomas Merton are reassuring. In *Contemplative Prayer,* Merton writes that

> our knowledge of God is paradoxically a knowledge not of him as the object of our scrutiny, but of ourselves as utterly dependent on his saving and merciful knowledge of us. . . . We know him in and through ourselves in so far as his truth is the source of our being and his merciful love is the very heart of our life and existence.

"By meditation," Merton remarks, "I penetrate the inmost ground of my life, seek the full understanding of God's will for me, of God's mercy to me, of my absolute dependence upon him."

Merton describes the aim of prayer much as we have described the aim of praying our experiences: "to come to know him through the realization that our very being is penetrated with his knowledge and love for us." We know God, Merton adds, "in so far as we become aware of ourselves as known through and through by him." Here Merton describes prayer not so much as coming to know God or reaching to love God but rather as realizing that we are known and loved by God. That realization, I believe, rises vividly to consciousness as we enter into the process of praying our experiences.

Karl Rahner, in *Christian at the Crossroads,* puts the matter clearly when he suggests that speaking of prayer as a dialogue with the Totally Other is difficult to conceive if we understand dialogue to mean messages uttered by God as an outside source. Sudden impulses and insights in prayer, Rahner reminds us, might be explained as coming from our own psychic powers. For many persons, therefore, the notion of dialogue in prayer seems to be the same as talking to ourselves. Rahner suggests that the concept of prayer as dialogue with the Totally Other can be more intelligible if we understand that "in prayer we experience ourselves as the ones spoken by God, as the ones arising from and decreed by God's sovereign freedom in the concreteness of our existence." In this way of understanding prayer, "we are ourselves . . . the utterance and address of God which listens to itself." In *Contemplative Prayer,* Merton expresses the same notion when he remarks, "I am myself a word spoken by God."

This means that in prayer we are neither on the one hand dialoguing with an outside source who utters messages from without, nor are we simply talking to ourselves. We are reaching deeply into ourselves and sensing more clearly that we are in God's knowledge and love. We are discovering the Divine within us. We are experiencing ourselves and our lives as uttered by God, and we listen.

This listening is not a narcissistic activity because we are not simply listening to our own ego. Rather, we are opening ourselves to that dimension of our being and experience in which God speaks. We are not talking to ourselves in such a way that we are consciously controlling and manipulating our reflection.

When we speak of prayer as dialogue, then, we are referring to encountering those levels of ourselves and of our experiences that we do not control because we have not formed them. They are not ours. We do not, in fact, even realize their existence until they manifest themselves. We do not possess these levels of experience; rather, at these levels we are possessed—possessed by God's deep abiding love. The ego in narcissism cannot enter here, for the ego carries the baggage of ambition and fear, of defensiveness and schemes, which cannot be allowed at this level of self-knowledge.

In the Book of Genesis, God utters the word and Creation springs forth. Today we are that word. Each of us is uttered in the uniqueness and actuality of our personal history. Our task is to hear that word as it wells up in us from our being and experience. We listen to the word with love and fear as we let it speak from our depths. Of what does the word speak? It speaks of the giftedness of our life; it speaks of the brokenness of our life. It fills us with awe of God's blessings, and it calls us to deeper purity and love toward God and all creation. It reverberates with the word of the Scriptures, which often helps us on our journey inward, but it now has the quality of our own unique and historical actuality.

6. Sacred Scripture:
Biblical Events and Personal History

IN OUR TRADITION all of the Scriptures are sacred to us, but only a small fraction stir and capture us. Some passages arouse in us such an emotional reaction that they cry out to be heard, and we cannot be free of them. These passages have such power over us because they touch a part of us that reverberates with their message. These passages stir and capture us not because they are special in themselves but because they have connected with a part of ourselves created by an experience now struggling to be unfolded. Scriptural passages that might have meant little to us before suddenly become a powerful force because they light up and refocus our experiences.

The incident of Philip in the Gospel of John (1:43–46) illustrates how an experience can be illuminated by the Scriptures. Philip had, no doubt, read the Torah with reverence from his youth; yet only after his experience of encountering Jesus did the Scriptures come alive for Philip. Indeed, they became the light illuminating Philip's experience of Jesus. Until then the Scriptures had lacked the compelling force that now they possessed for him. Philip sought out Nathanael, with whom he shared his enthusiasm: "We have found him of whom Moses in the Law and the prophets wrote, Jesus son of Joseph, from Nazareth" (John 1:45).

Another example of the Scriptures serving as a way into the depths of an experience is the account of the two disciples on the road to Emmaus (Luke 24:13–35). After that terrible and disheartening Friday, they were downcast. A stranger who had caught up to them as they walked consoled them by recalling to them passages from the Scriptures that referred to the Messiah. "Then, starting with Moses and going through all the prophets, he explained to them the passages throughout the scriptures that were about himself" (Luke 24:27). No doubt the disciples had heard these Scriptures before without being captured by them. Even now, although they listened intently, they were not aware of the compelling power the word was having on them. But after the stranger had vanished, the Scriptures flamed, and they realized their heart had been burning within them as the stranger explained the Scriptures on the way. The Scriptures had illuminated and refocused that profound Friday experience, and they ran to tell the others.

As we read the Scriptures, some passages kindle our heart. Our emotional response is our clue that a particular passage is addressed to us in a special way at this time in our life. We might have read the passage a hundred times before, but now it calls clearly and decisively. We are ready to be led into the depths of an experience, and the Scriptures will serve as our light.

Both for Philip and for the disciples on the road to Emmaus, the Scriptures served as a light on their experience. They could then turn from the Scriptures to explore and treasure their experience. They in a literal way found in their experience what we in a symbolic way also encounter: the presence and the call of the Lord. As with Philip and the disciples, the Scriptures serve us by illuminating, clarifying, and evaluating our experiences. Often, like a true friend, the Scriptures reach into our heart to arouse and to console by bringing out into the open memories and feelings that we might have scarcely known were there. These memories and feelings become the passage into the presence of the Lord in our life. The Scriptures call us, not to focus on the scriptural passages themselves, but to open ourselves to the Lord who lives and walks with us today.

Sometimes our respect for the Scriptures is so profound that we feel uneasy as we turn our attention from them to our experience. But in respecting them as a privileged expression of the word of God, we should not fail to respect also our own experience as a privileged expression of that same word of God. When we realize that the Scriptures themselves were written out of the experiences of the sacred authors and the community, we begin to view the events in our own life with more reverence. The God who is revealed through the events recounted in the Scriptures is also revealed in our daily life. This awareness makes less problematic our reflection on personal experiences as a way of knowing God's word for us.

The sacred Scriptures were written within a given culture for a particular audience with a specific theological language and imagery. These situations have changed since the Scriptures were composed, and so we could not expect our experiences of God to duplicate those recorded in the Bible. Our experiences today have the mark of our personal and communal lives within a particular culture at a particular time. But we can expect the sacred writings to shed light on our experiences and to help us explore and critique them.

The people of Israel sometimes confused their religious belief that God was faithful with their more rational hope that God would be consistent with their own understanding of history. We sometimes fall into the same trap. We can expect our experiences of God's call in our life to be in accord with God's call to Israel, but we would do ourselves an injustice to assume that there will be no surprises in our life. One of the consistent elements of God's call to Israel was the invitation to accept the unexpected: "Your ways are not my ways" (Isaiah 55:8).

A closed attitude to how God might be present in our life forces us to do violence to our experiences, just as such a closed attitude caused the Pharisees to reject and do violence to their experience of Jesus. Their misguided allegiance to a narrow understanding of the Scriptures and tradition resulted in their missing God present among them. The Pharisees assumed that any experience of the Messiah would fit their understanding of the Scriptures. They filtered personal experience through their reading of the holy word. We can be victims of the same dangerous possibility if we fail to open ourselves to receiving the Lord in our daily life.

Mary and the Apostles read the same holy writings as the Pharisees, but they did not use the writings to prejudge their experiences. Mary and the Apostles placed a supreme value on being available whenever and however God might call. In practice, they reverenced their experiences and allowed them to become the path along which they walked with the Lord.

The Scriptures serve us best not when they become a filter through which we prejudge our experiences but when they become our light and mirror. As our light, the Scriptures help us to clarify and explore our experiences. As our mirror, they help us to discover aspects of our experiences that previously have been inaccessible to our gaze. Neither a light nor a mirror is used to best advantage if it is looked at for its own sake. Rather, both are most helpful as a means of illuminating and exploring. If we find ourselves using the Scriptures as an excuse for not exploring and treasuring our own experiences, then we can suspect that we do not understand the very best of the Good News: that God is lovingly present to us in our daily living.

By praying our experiences, we come to know God's loving action in our daily life. We can then begin to focus on these experiences as the content of our offering to the Lord. Frequently we will be led to understand more fully a particular experience by the light of the Scriptures because the Scriptures can arouse us to the importance of an event and can move us into the depths of that experience. The Scriptures, however, will be misused in prayer if they cause us to do violence to our experience or to place no value on it. So, in praying our experiences, we need to use passages of the Scriptures to lead us back to our actual experiences, to illuminate them, and to enable us to explore and treasure them. In this way we may come closer to awareness of God's action in our life today.

7. Incarnational Prayer:
Praying from Our Humanness

A T THE HEART of Christian prayer resides the central mystery of Christianity, the Incarnation: "The Word became flesh and lived among us" (John 1:14).

The Incarnation holds this central place in prayer not only in the sense that we pray to the Father through and in and with the Word made flesh, but also because our own humanness, having been taken on by the Son of God, is the womb of our prayer. As Jesus, now "seated at the right hand of the Father," continues to share all the aspects of humanity with the Father, so our own sharing with the Father flows out of our human lives. As Jesus is united with the Father in humanness, we are drawn by the Spirit of Jesus to the Father in our humanness. The meaning and the hope of the mystery of the Incarnation, consummated in the Resurrection-Ascension, points to the truth that humanness is incorporated into godliness.

Through the Incarnation human life becomes for God an experience. God is not a spectator to human life; but, as Saint Paul says so emphatically, the Son of God *knows* our state; he knows in the biblical sense of knowing through intimate experience. God knows human life not only from having created it but from having lived it. The Word by which creation took place became flesh in order to enjoy and to agonize as a human being, to play and to cry, to experience the life and death patterns of humans in the midst of creation. The mystery of the Incarnation assures us that God is at home in humanness, and the mystery of the Resurrection-Ascension further assures us that humanness is at home in the Godhead.

"The Word became flesh and lived among us." It is clear in the Gospel that the Son of God lived human life not in some kind of pretense or in an otherworldly style but "in the flesh." An early Christian heresy held that Jesus only looked like a human being, that he posed as a man. Very few hold that idea today, but too few reflect on what it might mean that the Son of God experienced human life with all its messiness and sadness and fear, as well as its love and joy and beauty.

What might these considerations have to do with our prayer?

For many of us, in our efforts to develop our relationship with God, humanness seems to be part of the problem. We wish that we did not have human difficulties. We wish that we did not have to struggle with this or that human predicament. We want to rise above our humanness. We take the soaring impulses of our spirit to mean that our humanness, with all its finiteness, stupidity, and foolishness, is too limited and too ungodly to be of value. There is often a curious and subtle wish to be angelic.

Sometimes we deny our humanness; sometimes we reject our humanness; mostly we are quietly afraid of it—of the uncontrollability of its demands, of its limitations and inevitable slide to death. We are simply embarrassed about our humanness and wish that it would go away. We wish that our human concerns were over so that we could pray.

But the Incarnation tells us that our subtle desire to become angelic and rid ourselves of human concerns is a way of not meeting the Word on the Word's own ground: human life. The mystery of the Incarnation means that human concerns are concerns to God, and that our task is to accept and appreciate human life as human life and not to reject it as lesser angelic life. Jesus came that we would have this human life, with abundance, not with embarrassment or fear or reluctance.

Christian prayer is, then, not an attempt to move out of mundane human life but rather to enter into it more fully. Both the way of our prayer and the content of our prayer are to be not otherworldly but very much this-worldly. That is why, perhaps, one of the earliest Christian traditions about prayer spoke of prayer as not having been finished until the lips moved. That also may be why the earliest Christian forms of prayer were so involved in the physical: gestures, bodily movements, pilgrimages, processions, all surrounded with the sensualness of icons, candles, incense, and the touching of statues and beads.

We may look at these practices as primitive or unsophisticated, but we cannot afford to lose the fleshiness, the incarnationality, of our prayer. Some forms of prayer— for example, trying to rid ourselves of all our thoughts of human concerns so as to think only of God—may be a way that we vent our feelings of embarrassment about our human life. We sometimes suppose that prayer has to do with having lofty thoughts and wonderful ideas about God. But if our prayer is the raising of our human mind and our human heart to God, then we can hardly presume that our prayer will contain only lofty thoughts.

The reality of the Word having become flesh and having lived among us assures us that God is at home in human experience and that our prayer is born from our human experience. In particular it suggests that, at least at certain times in our life or in certain circumstances, we may find that the contents of our prayer, what we share with God in prayer, what is on our mind and in our heart raised to God, will be more explicitly rooted in our human experience. It suggests that we may at times be called to pray our experiences.

The story of the disciples on the road to Emmaus is a fine example of what praying our experiences might be for us who are disciples of the Word made flesh as we go our way on the road of life (see Luke 24:13–34). The risen Jesus comes to us as he did to those original disciples on the road to Emmaus, unrecognized; and taking the initiative, he asks us to share with him what are the concerns of life: "What are you discussing as you go your way?" We, like those disciples, may resist because, like them, we may be confused or embarrassed about our foolish or cowardly role in those concerns.

The disciples were distressed. They did not want to share their story, and they focused their feelings of resistance in the form of a counterquestion: "Are you the only one who does not know the things that have happened in Jerusalem?" But Jesus was not to be resisted. He insisted: "What things?"—tell me about yourself; let me share your distress, your confusion, all aspects of your experience; let me hear your story, so that I can increase your faith and trust. And when the disciples began to share their humanness with Jesus, and hear his reply, their hearts, their very selves, were ignited. They were filled with faith and became proclaimers of faith in the risen Christ.

What Jesus asks of his disciples in this story is what he seems to ask constantly of us in his desire for intimacy. That is, that we share with him our concerns, our feelings, the events of our life; that we pray our experiences. We deepen our relationship with God in prayer by sharing with God what, in fact, is happening in our human life.

Praying our experiences includes, of course, praying *about* our life situations. We say the Lord's Prayer for world peace, we offer a Hail Mary for a sick friend, we say the Serenity Prayer to help us through the next hour, or we pray a psalm in thanksgiving for a special grace. But praying our experiences particularly focuses on exploring with the risen Lord, as simply as did the disciples on the road, the significance of the events of our life. We share with the Word made flesh our own experience of what it is to be fleshy.

The reality of the Incarnation assures us that human concerns are God's concerns, and therefore invites us to look upon our prayer as a lifting to God of our mind and heart filled with those human concerns. From our humanness our prayer is born. In prayer, empowered by the Spirit of Truth, we share our story with the Lord as did the disciples on the road to Emmaus. Perhaps at first we share it with some inner struggle, but then in a deepening self-knowledge we come to an acceptance of our experiences, and finally we are gifted with an appreciation and gratitude for our life and ourselves as we really are in the hands of God. Then we, like the disciples, can authentically proclaim faith in the Word made flesh now risen and seated at the right hand of the Father.

8. Ministry:
Good Works, Love, and Ambiguity

S AINT JOHN BAPTIST DE LA SALLE, founder of the apostolic congregation of Brothers of the Christian Schools and himself considerably gifted in prayer, emphasized the value of doing good works as a means to spiritual growth. Although he encouraged his brothers to deeper levels of prayer, De La Salle was realistic enough to know that the brothers engaged in the ministry of education would often be preoccupied with their daily activities even during their time of prayer. He understood, moreover, that this preoccupation need not be a distraction but could serve as the content of prayer.

De La Salle directed his teaching brothers to incorporate reflection about their ministry into their meditation. In his *Meditations for the Time of Retreat,* he remarks: "You must constantly represent the needs of your [students] to Jesus Christ, explaining to him the difficulties you experience in guiding them." De La Salle would certainly have his brothers pray for their students, asking God to give them the graces to avoid sin. But, further, he would have his brothers directly reflect on, as a form of prayer, their work in the schools. He recommended that the brothers speak to the Lord about their recurring difficulties in correcting their students.

A brother's memories of his angry reaction to a problem student, or his feelings of weakness and conflict as he tried to correct a student, or the pain of his attempts at reconciliation, or the indecisiveness of his efforts to divert a student from selfishness—these memories and feelings are to be laid out and explained to the Lord. The brother's prayer, therefore, might consist of unfolding these memories and feelings and allowing them to bring him to a deeper awareness of his motives, his values, his weaknesses, his power of love, and his force of hate.

De La Salle constantly returned to the need for the brothers to integrate their work and prayer, and praying experiences was one of the ways De La Salle understood the integration of ministry and prayer to take place. It was also one of the ways he believed the brothers would come to understand and purify their motives.

De La Salle warned, as have all the masters of the spiritual life, that we ought to be cautious of our best intentions. Those who reflect seriously on their good works often come to see the ambiguity of their motivations. De La Salle recommends to those in ministry:

> Examine before God how you are acting in your ministry and whether you are failing in any of your responsibilities. Come to know yourself just as you are. Find fault with yourself accurately, unsparingly, so that when Jesus Christ comes to judge you, you will be able to face his judgment without being afraid.

We come to know ourselves just as we are when we reflect with honesty and openness on our experiences. To "examine before God how you are acting" is to enter the path of praying your experiences. It is a different way of saying what Teresa says about being sustained by the bread of the awareness of one's sins.

When we were adolescents, we believed that loving people was a rather simple thing. Now that we are adults and have engaged in many good works and entered many relationships, we may be aware that we have seldom loved anyone. It is painful to realize our conflicting purposes and our selfishness, but it is also a nourishing awareness—for this honesty brings us closer to the true self we wish to accept and offer to the Lord.

When we were young, we might have felt that we could easily do good works for God. It was, we might have imagined, only a matter of training and good intentions. Now that we are older, we may be aware that most of our works have been done at least in part for ourselves. To gain status among our colleagues, to exert power over those with whom we were working, to express a talent for organization in our specialty—these might have been the motivations that have produced our successful project. People have praised us for our good works, and we cannot deny that our works have helped others to live more human and faithful lives. We cannot reject as evil our desire to develop our own talents or to express our power of efficiency and organization. On the other hand, we know the ambiguity of our motivation, and as we come to know ourselves as we are, we are invited to "acknowledge our nothingness and abandon ourselves like a child into the arms of our good Lord." In such abandonment we "will be able to face his judgment without being afraid."

Involvement in doing good works is sometimes experienced as an obstacle to prayer. This will not be the case when our relationship to ministry and our experiences in ministry become the content of our prayer. As we pray our experiences of ministry, we resolve the dichotomy we may feel between works and prayer. Our ministry ceases to be a distraction to prayer and becomes the nourishment of prayer. Our work becomes the content of our prayer as our life becomes the focus of our offering to the Lord in faith.

9. Faith:
Incarnation and Truth

CARL JUNG wrote that he understood the greatest sin of faith to be that faith precludes experience. Jung was rightly rejecting a narrow view of faith. For some people faith does preclude experience, and we have seen that for others the Scriptures have that same effect. However, we should be suspicious of anything—even an understanding of faith or the Scriptures or prayer—that suggests that we devalue the concrete, everyday realities in our life. Incarnational faith, which is Christian faith, proclaims that in our unique and personal history, God is active.

If faith meant solely and simply assent to certain doctrines, then faith would tend to distort and preclude experience. If faith meant that we held certain truths even in the face of developing knowledge and growing experience, then faith would be the negative force Jung rejected. But if we more rightly understand that by faith we do not hold truths so much as we are held by Truth, then faith calls us into our experiences and is a way of being present to them, a way of entering into their depths with trust and thanksgiving. Faith calls us not to preclude our experiences but to include them in the Good News.

To what does faith call us through reflection on our experiences? Primarily we are called to realize in ourselves the Good News: that God is lovingly present to us here and now. We are called to search out in our ordinary and confusing personal and communal history the truth that we glibly affirm in theory: that God's life flows into our life. In particular, we are called to become aware of our helplessness and brokenness on the one hand, and God's blessings and love on the other. We are called to realize that we are weak and sinful, limited and broken, yet blessed and graced and gifted. We are called to "acknowledge our nothingness and abandon ourselves like a child into the arms of our good Lord."

Our life history is the clay out of which this realization is fashioned. We are called to take our personal history seriously. The joys and struggles, the care and hurt (both given and received), are all testimonies from our everyday life that God is in our life and that we can trust ourselves in the presence of the Lord. We are invited to unfold these experiences and to let God's loving presence come through for our praise and gratitude. We are asked to offer ourselves to God as the person who has lived the history that is ours and who has felt the personal experiences of brokenness and giftedness.

Sometimes a striking experience may startle us into an awareness of brokenness or blessedness. The death of a friend brings us to a realization of the preciousness of love and the beauty of friendship. We are also brought up short by an awareness of how shot through with narcissism our love has been. We recall the many acts of petty jealousy and the missed occasions when an affirmation or word of intimacy would have healed. We experience now in this death what Tillich called a sure sign of our sinfulness: we recall the times when we rejoiced even in the suffering of our dearest friend. We experience, too, in the death of one we struggled to love, our own mortality and the pressing weight of our own death. These realizations strike with clarity and force. When they come upon us, we have come under God's word judging us in our sinfulness and calling us to deeper integrity.

An experience of beauty and joy or a moment of intimacy may also put us in touch with an awareness of God's love and blessing. We ride on a mountain road, or walk along a beach, or experience the affection and complete acceptance of a friend, and we are suddenly awake to the realization that at work in our life is a force of love and care that fully encompasses us and all of reality. We see more clearly that we are loved quite undeservedly not just by a friend but by Life. We become more aware that we and all of creation are being sustained and nourished by a beneficent free Love. And in this we realize God's word uttered in blessing and care.

We could call experiences of such clarity and force "religious experiences" or "faith experiences" and then refer to other more ordinary experiences as "secular experiences." But this kind of distinction does not hold up. The experiences of God's presence under the aspects of judgment or love may come upon us most vividly in unique moments that are themselves gifts, but God's word and presence are also available in the depths of all of our experiences. We would be closer to the truth to speak of the "religious or faith dimension" of every experience.

God is addressing us in all moments of life. We may experience some moments as more privileged than others because they reveal with more clarity and force our limitations and our giftedness. That this revelatory power is more apparent in some moments than others is due more to our own openness and readiness than to the intensity and availability of God's saving presence.

Saint Teresa, too, referred to experience as revelatory of God's word. "Experience is a great help in all," she wrote in her autobiography, "for it teaches what is suitable for us; and God can be served in everything." And Saint Thérèse said the same more succinctly, following Saint Paul: "All is grace."

Our task, then, is to become aware of those obstacles of egoism that block the truth of our experiences and to allow those obstacles to be purged by the Truth. Our faith calls us to search our experiences, to preclude none of them, to relish all of them, trying to reach that limit, that depth where the sound of God's word of judgment and grace will become clear.

10. Our Best Prayer:
Summary and Encouragement

A FRIEND OF MINE, a religious sister, says that as a teenager she was not very good at sports, but like all the other teenagers in her all-girl school, she had to have a certain number of credits in physical education to graduate. She dreaded the thought of having to do exercises in gym class, and knew for certain that she never could actually learn to play any sport.

Fortunately for her, the school gym was being renovated that year and the physical-education class had to be held in an ordinary classroom. So thirty-five girls sat in rows of desks, some taking notes, some just with their hands folded, as the teacher taught them basketball. The teacher wrote on the board the definition of a dribble, a hook shot, and a fade-away jumper; and detailed the advantages of a fast break and a box defense. The girls listened attentively and read from the biographies of some basketball stars. The sister telling me this story said she didn't touch a basketball all year, she didn't even see a game, but she got an A in basketball. That's learning *about* something without ever being involved or doing it.

There is much these days to help us learn *about* prayer. There are many books about prayer and about those in the Christian tradition who have been noted for their prayer. There are lectures, workshops, and academic courses on prayer. And much stress is placed today on "techniques" of prayer: bodily postures, breathing exercises, and sequences of thoughts or images, which are offered to help us with prayer. All of these may indeed be helpful; they may be informative and inspiring, but at some point we get the feeling that we are sitting at a desk listening instead of being on the basketball court playing the game.

Wanting to know *about* prayer for the sake of intellectual interest, curiosity about how other people pray, or searching out information about techniques of prayer is like wanting to know *about* love. There is much to know about love, things that we can find inspiring in the lives of people who love, even some good that could come from knowing techniques of lovemaking—but all of this is quite different from actually loving.

The real issue about loving is not whether we have studied it enough academically or whether we know all the techniques, but who we are as loving persons and who we are called to be. There are no techniques for loving that we can learn before we actually love; all our unique ways of loving we know in retrospect. In this sense, there are no infallible techniques to prayer that will lead to a deeper relationship with God; there is only the longing of the heart to follow where prayer leads.

If we want to deepen our relationship with God, we must be in touch with our heart, in which the Spirit of love already resides. And similar to our experience of trying to love a human being, our prayer is a personal, unique, and above all, creative experience that unfolds as we come to know ourselves in the presence of God.

An American young man went to India in search of spiritual growth and came under the guidance of a famous guru. The young man lived with the guru for a number of weeks, and one day while the two were out walking beside a quiet lake, the young man found courage to ask the question, "How do I find God?" The guru looked at the young man in astonishment and said, "There are no methods to finding God; follow your heart."

The young man insisted that there must be techniques, shortcuts, practices. The guru shook his head and then suddenly jumped on the young man, caught him quite off balance, threw him to the ground, dragged him to the edge of the lake, and thrust his head under the water. The young man was shocked when he sensed that he was being held under the water by a strong and determined set of hands and was, in truth, drowning. He struggled, but to no avail. He grew panicky, and lunged with all his might until he finally managed to get his head out of the water, and crawled away exhausted.

Shocked and still gasping for breath, the young man screamed at the guru, "You tried to drown me." The guru said, "When you seek union with God with the same intensity that you are gasping for air, then you will find God." There are no techniques for finding God, for deepening prayer; accomplishing this is a matter of making it the desire of our life and then allowing ourselves to be led.

There are ways of personal prayer that have developed over centuries and that we come to know by studying the tradition of prayer. But these ways are intended to inspire us and not to replace the way of prayer that comes to us as we actually pray. To come to know our unique way of prayer is not to disregard the tradition but to respond to the tradition. One of the wisest bits of traditional advice about prayer is simply this: "Pray the way you can and not the way you can't." Sometimes studying prayer as a subject leads us to want to pray the way that is recommended by a teacher or a book, for whatever reason. True, we can be informed and even inspired by others, but our prayer is fundamentally unique and can only become known to us as we actually pray.

All of this implies that our prayer will develop as we strive to be honest with ourselves about who we are in the presence of God. As we share with God what at any given moment we know to be our truth, we are really participating in the movement of the Spirit of Truth already praying within us. And that is our best prayer.

Let us summarize our discussion of the concept of praying our experiences by briefly considering four notions: praying from our heart; telling our story to God; opening ourselves to receive God's Spirit, the Spirit of Truth; and, finally, coming to spiritual self-knowledge.

Praying from our heart. Jesus' own teachings on prayer seem to emphasize that if prayer is not to be hypocritical, it must come from our heart rather than only from our lips. Prayer originating in the heart may do well to end up on the lips, but prayers originating on the lips can be merely words without heart. Jesus assured his disciples that when they came to prayer, they did not need to heap words on words as the pagans did, for what is important is not the abundance, nor even the precision, of the words, but that the words carry the heart. It is the heart raised to God that matters; the prayer carries the heart.

The Hebrew Scriptures speak of God as not needing sacrifices of burnt offerings, or holocausts of any kind, but longing for the offering of a contrite and humble heart. God's request that we offer our heart is, of course, a personal invitation to return love for love. It is another way of saying what Jesus will say when he invites his disciples on the road to Emmaus to open their hearts to him by sharing their experiences. The point of prayer is to offer to God our authentic selves. The heart, contrite and humble, is a symbol of that open and honest sharing with God of the essence and totality of who we really are.

But it is not always easy to be ourselves in the presence of God. Sometimes we wish we were someone else, someone more noble or important, someone less weak and unworthy. Sometimes we might even wish that parts of ourselves would simply cease to exist—that we could just blot out certain parts of ourselves and our experiences. But God wants our heart even if it is heavy and broken. God wants us fully as we are, in the authenticity of our present situation.

Telling our story to God. When our heart is present, when we are really there, so to speak, then we can share ourselves with God; otherwise there is an aspect of the hypocritical, the unreal, the phony that contaminates our relationship with God. When we are really present to ourselves, then we can explore, in the presence of God, the meaning of our life, the significance of our unrest, our joys, our fears, our hopes. In short, when we are in touch with our heart, then we can share our personal story with God in prayer.

One of the common ways in which the Hebrew Scriptures refer to prayer is under the image of story-telling. Traditionally the celebration of the Passover became the occasion for the people to tell their story. This greatest of ceremonial prayers was the occasion when the people, fully in touch with who they were, lifted their hearts and told the story of God's great blessings to them. They told the story of their being chosen, their attempts to respond, their triumphs, their failures, their hopes, their joys, their sorrows, and always God's fidelity. Telling their story was their prayer.

The prophets, too, prayed by telling the people the story of God's concern and fidelity in the present situation. The prophets prayed their own experiences, also, as those experiences revealed God's continuing call to them and to the people. They prayed out of the situation in which they found themselves. Sometimes they prayed in anger, in confusion, in despair, but always in the desire to know themselves and God's call.

The Psalms also are basically prayers in which the story of the people is told and retold in poetic praise, sorrow, joy, and hope. In fact, the entire corpus of sacred Scripture is the recounting of the stories of the people in their efforts to make sense of their lives, to respond to God's call, to live in God's presence.

In the ceremonial storytelling of the Passover, in the personal storytelling of the prophets, in the response to Christ of the disciples on the way to Emmaus, in the communal telling of the story in the Psalms and other books of the sacred Scriptures, what was important was not that the words were proper or that the sentiments were exalted or refined or even that the story was flattering. What was important was that an attempt was made to be truthful in the telling. In praying our experiences, we tell God our personal story in all its aspects as honestly as we can. In this kind of prayer, we answer the Lord's question: "What things?" (Luke 24:19).

Opening ourselves to receive God's Spirit, the Spirit of Truth. As we pray from our heart in the telling of our story to God, we are already under the influence of the Holy Spirit, who alone empowers us to be honest in seeking intimacy with God. Jesus assured his Apostles at the Last Supper that when he went to the Father, he would send them the Holy Spirit, who is the Spirit of Truth. Saint Paul testifies to the fulfillment of this promise from his own experience and tells us that we do not even know how to pray as we ought but that the Holy Spirit prays in us in ways we do not even know. The Spirit of Truth moves us to open ourselves to find the truth of our experiences.

In praying our experiences, we open to God our story with as much truth as we can muster. Of course, our struggle is always to share our story without distortion, without manipulating the data so as to make our story appear more proper or more grand. Elements of our story always threaten us with their revelation of our own foolishness and stupidity, our greed and our jealousy. To begin to share our story with God with as much truth as we can afford is a gift given by the Spirit, who is already acting within us.

At the same time, sharing our story with God is also a call from that Spirit to see the distortions in our telling, to be aware of the subtle deceit whereby we make our story just a bit more acceptable to ourselves. It is a call to be more honestly ourselves.

Jesus' promise to send us the Spirit of Truth is a promise to lead us to himself and to the Father—to the Truth. We cannot have any doubt that as we struggle to come to the truth of who we are and the truth of the meaning our experiences, we are, in fact, already praying.

Coming to spiritual self-knowledge. Many of the Christian saints over the centuries, including, as we have seen, Teresa of Ávila, referred to praying our experiences under the notion of coming to self-knowledge. She was, of course, not referring primarily to the self-knowledge that one could learn today from psychological tests. Such tests are useful for their own purposes, but they are based on categories invented by the test makers, and the test results are ultimately comparisons.

Rather, Teresa and the Christian saints were referring to a self-knowledge that comes to us as we open our heart in prayer. By being aware, in the presence of God, of who we take ourselves to be, a self-knowledge comes to us that is not based on comparisons. By simply being aware of all the elements of our experiences—while not attempting to decipher them or manage them or correct them and especially not attempting to critique them by any human categories—by simply being attentive to them in the presence of God, we come to a self-knowledge that is outside the range of human categories.

The truth that comes to us, the meaning that unfolds for us in prayer is not completely relevant to what the theoreticians have categorized in their understanding of human experience. The self-knowledge that is given to us by testing, however helpful that may be, ultimately tells us who we are in the hands of whoever developed the theory and invented the test. The truth that comes to us as we pray our experiences is the unique and incomparable truth of who we are in the hands of God.

Teresa speaks of this spiritual self-knowledge as the very beginning of prayer and also as so fundamental to prayer that we can never grow beyond it. We return often and always to this ground of self-knowledge. Such spiritual self-knowledge frees us into an acceptance and appreciation of our human life as it presently is in all its aspects. Categories we usually apply to our experiences—good and bad, desirable and undesirable, right and wrong—become somehow irrelevant. What is clear is that in God "we live and move and have our being" and that our experiences constitute the story of God's fidelity to us. And we know that that truth is enough.

Some people will recognize that what has been described here about praying our experiences is a method that they have used off and on for many years. These persons may not be able to articulate why reflecting on their experiences felt like prayer, but they know it has filled their times of prayer and has been a source of the strength, confrontation, growth, and peace that have traditionally been associated with prayer. They also know that in this process they have been in the presence of the Lord of their life.

These persons may find encouragement in continuing to pray their experiences. They may also begin to notice sources other than the Scriptures or formal religious exercises impelling them into the depths of their experiences.

Earlier I mentioned the power of a random remark to call us to pray our experiences. The death of a friend, the awareness of beauty, or an impulse of anger may also compel us to pray in this way. This same power may be found in the passages of a novel, in the imagery of a poem, in moments of personal joy or grief, in the scenes of a movie, in the beauty of music, in times of playfulness, in the sounds of nature, in the details of a news article. Persons who are sensitive to the call of ordinary life situations are privileged indeed because they are being invited to take seriously the truth that God "is not far from any of us, since it is in [God] that we live, and move, and exist" (Acts of the Apostles 17:28).

Our life, we profess, is lived in God. There is no doubt that we can find God in the depths and flow of our own experiences. On occasion we will have to take formal time for this kind of reflection, but ultimately it is in the very process of living our daily existence that we are called to find God's word and to offer ourselves in response. When we purify our stance toward life so that our narcissism is out of the way, and when at the center of our life are openness and reverence, then we will find one experience clarifying another, and all of our life revealing the caring presence of God and leading us to self-offering.

The greatest gift that we are asked to accept is the gift of living our life reverently. We are assured that Jesus came not that we may have more prayers, or more reading of the Scriptures, or more pious devotions, or more of anything, but only "that [we] might have life and have it more abundantly" (John 10:10, NAB).

Notes

21 Kieran Kavanaugh and Otilio Rodriguez, trans., *The Book of Her Life,* in *The Collected Works of St. Teresa of Ávila* (Washington, DC: ICS Publications, 1976), p. 94.

25 "if you think your little Thérèse . . .": F. J. Sheed, trans., *Collected Letters: St. Thérèse of Lisieux,* 2d ed. (London: Sheed and Ward, 1977), p. 114.
"Perfection seems easy . . .": Rev. Francois Jamart, *Complete Spiritual Doctrine of St. Thérèse of Lisieux,* trans. by Rev. Walter Van De Putte (New York: Alba House, 1961), p. 134.
"No book, no theologian . . .": Jamart, *Complete Spiritual Doctrine,* p. 31.

38 Jamart, *Complete Spiritual Doctrine,* p. 47.

39 Jamart, *Complete Spiritual Doctrine,* p. 65.

45 "our knowledge of God . . .": Thomas Merton, *Contemplative Prayer* (Garden City, NY: Doubleday and Company, Image Books, by special arrangement with Herder and Herder, 1971), p. 83.
"By meditation . . .": Merton, *Contemplative Prayer,* p. 68.

46 "to come to know him . . .": Merton, *Contemplative Prayer,* p. 83.
"in prayer we experience . . .": Karl Rahner, *Christian at the Crossroads* (New York: Seabury Press, 1975), p. 66.
"I am myself a word . . .": Merton, *Contemplative Prayer,* p. 68.

61 John Baptiste de La Salle, *Meditations for the Time of Retreat* (Romeoville, IL: Christian Brothers Conference, 1975), p. 56.

62 De La Salle, *Meditations,* p. 89.

68 "Experience is a great help . . .": Kavanaugh and Rodriguez, *Collected Works,* p. 83.

"All is grace.": Ida Friederike Görres, *The Hidden Face: A Study of St. Thérèse of Lisieux* (New York: Random House, Pantheon Books, 1959), p. 378.